KATE GREENAWAY

Curly Locks
The April Baby's Book of Tunes
1900 (7¼ x 7½ ins)

Kate Greenaway, 1880. From a photograph by Elliott & Fry

RODNEY K. ENGEN

KATE GREENAWAY

ACADEMY EDITIONS · LONDON
HARMONY BOOKS · NEW YORK

title page
Pen and ink line drawing
(7 x 5½ ins)

front cover
Detail from *May Blossom*
Under the Window
1878 (9¼ x 7¼ ins)

back cover
St. Valentine's Day
Watercolour, pen, ink
(Victoria and Albert Museum)

Frontispiece to the Extra Supplement *Illustrated London News,*
15th February 1879

ACKNOWLEDGEMENTS

I wish to thank Sir Charles Tennyson for his hospitality and
assistance; Mrs. Gee, Keeper of the Kate Greenaway Collection
Hampstead, and her assistant, for advice and permission to
photograph from the collection; Mrs. Maragret Maloney,
Librarian, The Osborne Collection, Toronto, for bibliographical
information; Mr. R. Green, Keeper of Fine Art, Laing Art
Gallery, Newcastle-upon-Tyne, for catalogue information;
Mr. Ralph Fastnedge, Curator, The Lady Lever Art Gallery, Port
Sunlight, for catalogue information; the Witt Library; the staff
of the Victoria and Albert Museum Print Room and Library;
Phillips Ltd. and the staff of the Swiss Cottage Reference Library,
London Borough of Camden.

R.E.

NOTE:

Dimensions given with illustrations from books and periodicals
indicate the overall page size and not those of the illustration.
All sizes are to the nearest quarter inch.

First published in Great Britain in 1976 by
Academy Editions 7 Holland Street London W8

First published in the U.S.A. in 1976 by Harmony Books,
a division of Crown Publishers, Inc., 419 Park Avenue South,
New York, New York 10016

Library of Congress Catalog Card Number 75-37388

Printed and bound in Great Britain by
William Clowes & Sons, Ltd., Beccles, Suffolk

Kate Greenaway's books and paintings were filled with a delicate charm that defined a fanciful world of Victorian sentimentality. She was a shrewd escapist who created a universal, sugar-coated world of sexless, middle-class children, dressed in derivative costumes, romping blissfully in idyllic pastel-coloured landscapes. Although she was a quiet unassuming spinster, undaunted by fame, her illustrated books, greeting cards and paintings set the standard for proper dress and manners; they were read and collected throughout the world and she became a fashionable institution. Indeed, her meticulously drawn children blended the Pre-Raphaelite spirit for detail with Aesthetic Movement stylishness and were aimed at the one previously neglected area of Victorian sentimentality—the nursery. Her work was consistently praised by noted contemporary critics—John Ruskin compared her greeting cards with Raphael, while others believed her flowers equalled those of Botticelli. She, however, continued to view the world through the eyes of the children she felt she knew, claiming: 'I hated to be grown-up, and cried when I had my first long dress. . .'

Curiously Kate Greenaway's work not only charmed the academic fine art world but also created a fashionable popular demand. She began her artistic career during the 1860s and '70s, a period marked by the re-emergence of interest in the eighteenth century which was manifested in the creation of Queen Anne-style architecture, represented by R. Norman Shaw's designs for the 'aesthetically aware' (he in fact designed Kate Greenaway's Hampstead studio-home); a revived Gainsborough-pastiche style in Millais, Orchardson, and Marcus Stone paintings; and the most extravagant revival of women's period fashions.

Kate Greenaway also developed the ability to portray a child's idealism, which her intimate friend, John Ruskin, described in his Slade lecture *Fairy Land* in 1883: '. . . till at last, out like one of the sweet Surrey fountains, all dazzling and pure, you have the radiance and innocence of re-instated infant divinity showered again among the flowers of English meadows by Mrs. Allingham and Kate Greenaway.' Ruskin believed children had been a neglected subject for artists of the past—a defect in Greek art as well as

thirteenth century Gothic art. Not, in fact, until the work of the Victorian painter Sir David Wilkie (1785-1841) were children painted as individuals. Children were important symbols, reminders to a rapidly industrialised society that the appreciation of quiet child-naivety, nature and fantasy were necessary: to Ruskin a Kate Greenaway design was therapeutic purity and beauty—where 'there are no railroads in it, to carry the children away with. . . no tunnel or pit mouths to swallow them up, no league-long viaducts, no blinkered iron bridges. . .' And 'the beauty of them is in *being* like. They are blissful, just in the degree that they are natural; and the fairy land she sees, creates for you, is not beyond the sky nor beneath the sea, but nigh you, even at your doors. She does but show you how to see it, and how to cherish.'

Victorians of all ages cultivated the escapist fantasies of fairies, myths and legends—the illustrations of Richard Doyle, Richard Dadd and Sir Noël Paton were extremely popular. Kate Greenaway began her magazine illustrations under their influence and made her debut exhibiting six fairy-story illustrations at the Dudley Gallery in 1868, which were subsequently published in *People's Magazine*. In his first letter to her in 1880, John Ruskin asked anxiously, 'Do you believe in fairies?' To Ruskin the fairy world represented a 'closeness of ocular distance'—a necessary microscopic view of the world to be painted from carefully observed natural forms similar to the Pre-Raphaelite manner. Indeed, Ruskin sent pieces of sod to Kate Greenaway for study and drawing. However, she lacked the imagination necessary to devise a very personal fairy-world; rather she believed in the enchantment of children and when Ruskin challenged her to draw a series of fairies she retorted: 'They'll be very like children. . .' Later she witnessed the decline in such escapism when in 1888 she wrote to an author: '. . . and people don't care much for tales of Fairies—now.'

As with the work of many Victorian artists, Kate Greenaway's designs were a successful borrowing from numerous often exotic elements of popular taste: she fell under the spell of a rising cult of aestheticism and was in fact a natural aesthete. But she disagreed with Walter Pater, the spiritual father of the aesthetic

philosophy, when he declared: 'I am partial to the meadow-sweet but on an evening like this there is too much of it. It is the fault of nature in England that she runs too much to excess.' On the contrary, Kate Greenaway never tired of admiring nature or drawing flowers and landscapes. And like Huysman's aesthete in his novel *A Rebours*, who preferred to remain in his own self-made environment, regulating every conceivable perception, she preferred to remain in the private world of her Hampstead studio and garden–she sketched her impression of her hermetic life in a letter to her friend Violet Dickinson. She cherished the sanctity of a quiet, sheltered life, and her work recorded the mere bits and pieces of a synthesized, often imagined, ideal beauty. Her work could be criticised for its superficial approach–recording only momentary prettiness in figures easily drawn and duplicated. Indeed, when interior views were needed she drew her studio; her father and brother modelled for her male figures; and she retained the same child models for many designs.

Kate Greenaway admired the work of her contemporaries, particularly Millais, Rossetti, Burne-Jones, Walter Crane and Lord Leighton (who bought two of her drawings in 1891). She was also aware of Whistler's controversial works and Beardsley's drawings (she wrote in 1894: 'Tell Mr. Ponsonby I *hate* Beardsley more than ever'). Curiously, Beardsley admired her work–at the age of eleven he earned £30 in six weeks drawing Greenaway figures on menu cards and guest placards. Walter Crane's superior illustrations left her feeling sadly depressed and inadequate and although their Valentine designs were published together in *The Quiver of Love* in 1876, they remained distant acquaintances. Crane wrote of her importance: '. . . the child-like spirit of her designs in an old-world atmosphere, though touched with conscious modern 'aestheticism', captivated the public in a remarkable way. . . I think she overdid the big bonnet rather, and at one time her little people were almost lost in their clothes.' The illustrator Randolph Caldecott was also an intimate friend who at one time was even mistaken for her husband.

Born at Hoxton in 1846, Kate Greenaway was a sensitive child from a middle-class family. Her father

was a hard-working wood-engraver, her mother ran a fancy goods shop in later years. Kate spent two idyllic years in a country farmhouse at Rolleston where she learned to love the cottages, fields and woods that later appeared in her illustrations. She drew from her father's collection of magazines (he engraved for *The Illustrated London News*), read popular children's books, studied the colour engravings of John Martin from the front of shop windows, and admired George Cruikshank's work. One in particular horrified her– Cruikshank's illustration of 'The Death of Edward Underhill' in Ainsworth's *The Tower of London* of 1840, which she kept hidden, returning to it from time to time, thus renewing her terror. As a diligent student at the chief school of the Art Department of South Kensington, she won medals for her decorative designs. She attended life classes at Heatherley's School and later entered the new London Slade School where she studied under the French Professor Alphonse Legros.

From the start, Kate Greenaway's attitude toward her work reflected her Victorian background–she was a diligent, hard-working student and with her friend Elizabeth Thompson (later the famous painter Lady Butler) would bribe the custodian to allow them extra hours in the drawing studio. She first exhibited a series of drawings on wood blocks in 1868 and subsequent illustrations were published in children's periodicals and *The Illustrated London News*. Demand for her work grew as she drew for children's novels, greeting cards and eventually her own books: her income increased from £70 in 1872 to £1500 in 1881. The early greeting card designs published by Marcus Ward and Company were a great financial success, issued at a time when major Royal Academicians were designing similar cards.

In 1878 Kate Greenaway began her working association with the pioneer colour engraver-printer Edmund Evans. In the same year he printed her first book *Under the Window* which was reprinted with foreign sales reaching a staggering hundred thousand copies. In addition he published a series of superior quality coloured children's Toybooks illustrated by Walter Crane and Randolph Caldecott. The demand for Greenaway designs resulted in copybook artists re-drawing her figures for painted china; decorators

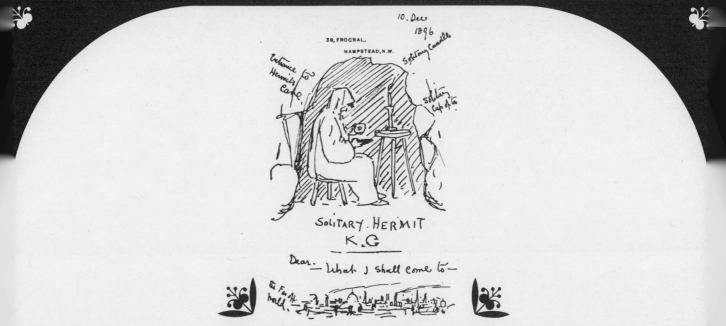

printed Greenaway-inspired wallpaper (the one product which she sanctioned); silversmiths stamped figures into cooking utensils, and dressmakers designed children's clothing in the style the French were to call *Greenawisme.*

Under the Window—written and illustrated by Kate Greenaway—was followed by *Kate Greenaway's Birthday Book for Children* in 1880, *A Day in a Child's Life* and *Mother Goose* in 1881, and in 1882 she illustrated *Little Ann and Other Poems* (a book she enjoyed as a child). She also did a series of illustrated *Almanacks for 1883-1897* (excluding 1896). *Language of Flowers* was published in 1884 followed by *Marigold Garden* in 1885 (considered the high point of her career), *A Apple Pie* in 1886, *The Pied Piper of Hamelin* (perhaps her finest attempt at historical illustration) and *The April Baby's Book of Tunes* in 1900.

These early books represented innovative examples of a colour printing process perfected by Edmund Evans: the original design was photographed onto specially prepared wooden blocks which were engraved with one block for each of the three colours used; the blocks were aligned so that the colour overlapping, or 'register', of the print produced a sharp new series of tones. Kate Greenaway's early black and white wood-engraved illustrations for *Little Folks* and *The Illustrated London News* were occasionally engraved by her father—these derived mainly from the style of engraved portraits of Swain and Tenniel. Soon her own delicate, finely drawn children became easily distinguishable, engraved with clear outlines and little shading. These designs were published as outline drawings suitable for painting in *The Little Folks Painting Book* in 1879. Ten years later the familiar 'KG' signature was replaced by the 'LL' of Lizzie Lawson, a successful copyist of Greenaway figures—her stylised designs of children were adapted for an oriental treatment in Julia Goddard's story *A Japanese Red Riding Hood* in *Little Folks* in 1889. The real success of Kate Greenaway's designs was due to their delicate lines and accurately reproduced colours (one critic called her drawings Flaxman-like). Ruskin wrote in his *Fairy Land* lecture: 'All great art is delicate; and fine to the uttermost. Wherever there is blotting, or

daubing, or dashing there is weakness at least; probably affectation; certainly bluntness of feeling.'

John Ruskin was a guiding force both as critic and friend throughout Kate Greenaway's life: he wrote some five hundred letters to her and she wrote nearly double that amount to him. He believed early on that she was wasting her talent making mere pictorial borders 'that glitter like unregarded gold' when she should be illustrating narratives: 'We must get her to organise a school of colourists by hand who can absolutely facsimile her own first drawing.'

Although her work was warmly praised, it did contain a number of glaring faults, many of which she tried to correct, others she realised were beyond her ability to change: she exaggerated the pointed chins of her children who appeared generally sexless; she drew their eyes too far apart; their limbs often did not appear connected to their bodies; their feet were too large or carelessly drawn. She never really mastered the technique of drawn perspective; drapery was often too studied and lacked grace and natural flow (a criticism which was also levelled against that pillar of classicism, Lord Leighton, whose draped figures resembled painted marble). Her paintings borrowed the genre settings of Fred Walker, G.D. Leslie and H. Stacey Marks, the idealism of G.F. Watts, the colour of Rossetti and the beauty of Burne-Jones and Millais. She exhibited consistently at the Dudley Gallery, the Royal Institute of Painters in Water Colour (she became a member in 1889), the Fine Art Society and the Royal Academy.

Kate Greenaway maintained a respect for literature throughout her life: she read constantly but indiscriminately, lacking a critical faculty. She began a series of illustrations interpreting scenes from Shakespeare published in *Little Folks* July 1877; she wrote the verses to many of her books as well as two volumes of sonnets on themes of Pre-Raphaelite intensity—her own unfulfilled love and self-sacrifice to her art. Tennyson and his family were her friends (an 1889 edition of his works was inscribed 'Kate Greenaway Tennyson'), and Frederick Locker, author of *London Lyrics,* was one of her most devoted friends and a great admirer of her verses. At the end of her life she began a series of projected illustrations to William Blake's

Songs of Innocence, but these were never completed.

In the early 1890s, Kate Greenaway shrewdly realised that her success in the art world was coming to an end. She turned, unsuccessfully, to oil portraiture in 1899; she considered dress designing (she had sewn costumes for her models from which she made her drawings); and was offered the editorship of a children's magazine. She even contemplated sculpture. 'It is so difficult now I am no longer at all the fashion,' she wrote to Ruskin in 1898. 'I say fashion for that is the right word, that is all it is to a great many people.' She also wrote a bitter poem:

> Deserted, cast away, my work all done,
> Who was a star that shone a little while,
> But fallen now and all its brightness gone—
> A victim of this world's fickle smile,
> Pool fool and vain, grieve not for what is lost,
> Nor rend thy heart by counting up the cost.

Kate Greenaway attempted to domesticate the world's children in her own, pointedly decent manner. She died in 1901, surviving the scandalous Aubrey Beardsley by three years. She had been a hard-working mousy little woman with a determination to portray goodness and beauty and a dedication to her art. Living during the anxious period of artistic eclecticism, she created in her work a unique nursery-rhyme fantasy where beauty and sentiment were the only nurses of very 'proper' children. Her books and designs helped dress the world's children. This surely must have given her great pleasure, as she wrote:

> There are sometimes moments, when I see
> A sort of divinity in it for me,
> To keep me separate and alone;
> To hold away and keep my heart
> All for my work, set aside and apart,
> As if I were vowed away to Art.

CAPTIONS TO TEXT ILLUSTRATIONS

page 5
Kate Greenaway. Engraved portrait

page 6
The Studio. 39, Frognal, Hampstead

page 7
Letter head sketch
To Miss Violet Dickinson, 10th December 1896

page 8
Dead. Watercolour sketch (5 x 7 ins)
For illustrated edition of sonnets written by Kate Greenaway, but never published

🐌 THE PLATES 🐌

Jack and Jill
The April Baby's Book of Tunes
1900 (7¼ x 7½ ins)

Petronel and Petronilla Escape in a Boat
Starlight Stories told to Bright Eyes and Listening Ears
1877 (6¾ x 5 ins)

Kate Greenaway's ability to draw fairies and goblins was first recognised by the editor of *The People's Magazine*, Rev. W.J. Loftie. He bought six drawings on wood of fairies, which she exhibited at the Dudley Gallery in 1868, and published them periodically from 1873.

The Fairy Rubinetta
Fairy Gifts or **A Wallet of Wonders**
1875 (6¾ x 5 ins)

The plates for this book were wood engraved by Kate Greenaway's father and praised for 'revealing a fine taste in witches and apparitions'.

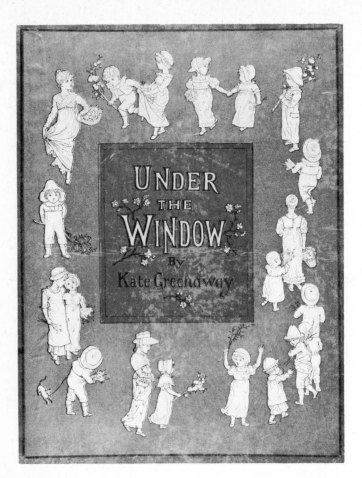

Four illustrations from **Under the Window**
1878 (9¼ x 7¼ ins)

This book was the first produced from Kate Greenaway's association with the London colour-printer, Edmund Evans, who also published the children's books of Walter Crane and Randolph Caldecott. The book's drawings were exhibited at the Fine Art Society in 1880 and applauded. The American journal *Literary World* of Boston claimed 'her delicacy and beauty of faces in outline as good as Flaxman; and the curious quality of affectionateness in the drawings, their prettiness that would have moved the heart of Stothard and touched the soul of Blake'.

THIS little fat Goblin,
  A notable sinner,
Stole cabbages daily,
  For breakfast and dinner.

The Farmer looked sorry;
  He cried, and with pain,
"That rogue has been here
  For his cabbage again!"

That little plump Goblin,
  He laughed, "Ho! ho! ha!"
Before me he catches,
  He'll have to run far."

That little fat Goblin,
  He never need sorrow;
He stole three to-day,
  And he'll steal more to-morrow.

YES, that's the girl that struts about,
  She's very proud,—so very proud!
Her *bow-wow*'s quite as proud as she:
They both are very wrong to be
  So proud—so very proud.

See, Jane and Willy laugh at her,
  They say she's very proud;
Says Jane, "My stars!— they're very silly;"
"Indeed they are," cries little Willy,
  "To walk so stiff and proud."

LITTLE boys and girls, will you come and ride
With me on my broomstick,—far and wide?
First round the sun, then round the moon,
And we'll light on the steeple, to hear a merry tune.

Frontispiece
Heartsease or **The Brother's Wife**
1879 (7½ x 4¾ ins)

Kate Greenaway illustrated this novel by Charlotte M. Yonge with three full-page
illustrations. She felt, however, that she should not illustrate other people's books
which limited her own imaginative abilities and abandoned this work after three
drawings.

Kate Greenaway's Birthday Book for Children
1880 (3¾ x 3½ ins)

The 12 colour plates and 382 drawings were printed by Edmund Evans in a first edition of 50,000.

Ride a cock-horse
Mother Goose or **The Old Nursery Rhymes**
1881 (6¾ x 4¾ ins)

This book was filled with her most delicate designs to date, although poor printing registers destroyed their meticulous qualities.

Mary, Mary Quite Contrary
Mother Goose or **The Old Nursery Rhymes**
1881 (6¾ x 4¾ ins)

Watercolour and pencil study from the original manuscript *(left)*
(Photograph: Courtesy Witt Library, London)

Final colour plate engraved and printed by Edmund Evans *(right)*

Back cover to **Little Ann and Other Poems**
1882 (9 x 6 ins)

The cover was the same back and front. The text poems by Jane and Ann Taylor were
first published in 1804-5 and were read by Kate Greenaway as a child.

THE GAUDY FLOWER.

WHY does my Anna toss her head,
   And look so scornfully around,
As if she scarcely deign'd to tread
   Upon the daisy-dappled ground?

Does fancied beauty fire thine eye,
   The brilliant tint, the satin skin?
Does the loved glass, in passing by,
   Reflect a graceful form and thin?

Little Ann and Other Poems
1882 (9 x 6 ins)

During her childhood in Islington, Kate Greenaway and her friends played 'pretence'—
a game of imagining their lives merged with those of the mysterious, nurse-guarded
children they met on walks.

THE ORPHAN.

My father and mother are dead,
   Nor friend, nor relation I know ;
And now the cold earth is their bed,
   And daisies will over them grow.

I cast my eyes into the tomb,
   The sight made me bitterly cry ;
I said, " And is this the dark room,
   Where my father and mother must lie ? "

Little Ann and Other Poems
1882 (9 x 6 ins)

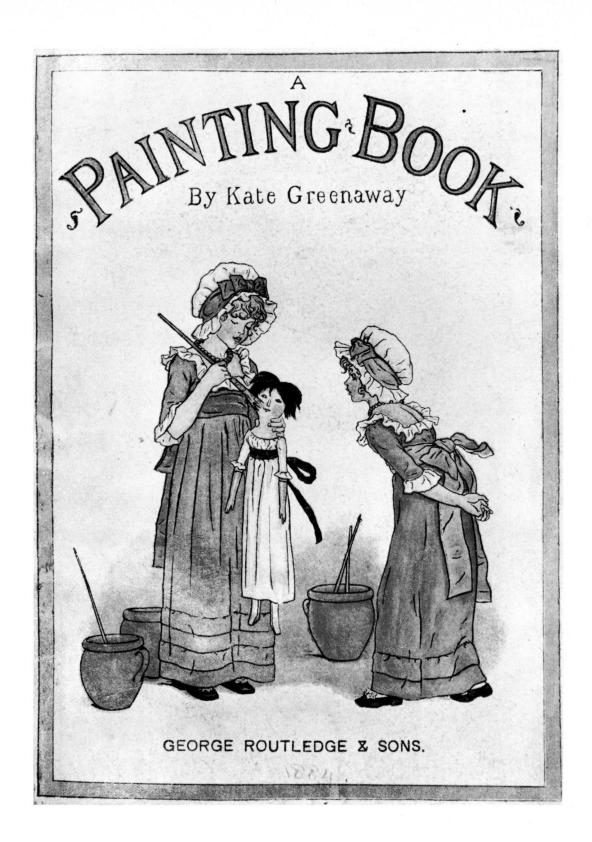

Cover to **A Painting Book**
1884 (9½ x 7¼ ins)

The book consisted of line block drawings borrowed from the publications *Under the Window, A Day in a Child's Life, Marigold Garden* and *Mother Goose*. Over 40,000 copies were printed.

First edition binding of **Language of Flowers**
1884
(Photograph: Courtesy Witt Library, London)

The book was printed in an edition of 19,500, half of which
went to America where collectors bound them in leather and
gold. Ruskin, however, criticised the book: 'You are at present
working wholly in vain. There is no joy and very, very little
interest in any of these flower book subjects, and they look as
if you had nothing to paint them with but starch and camomile
tea.'

Language of Flowers
1884 (9 x 4¾ ins)

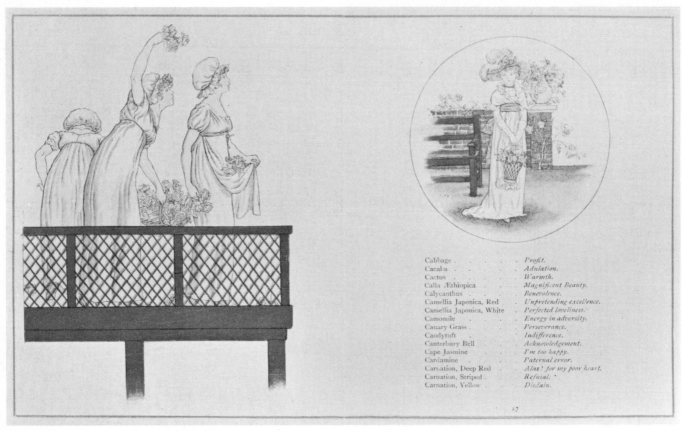

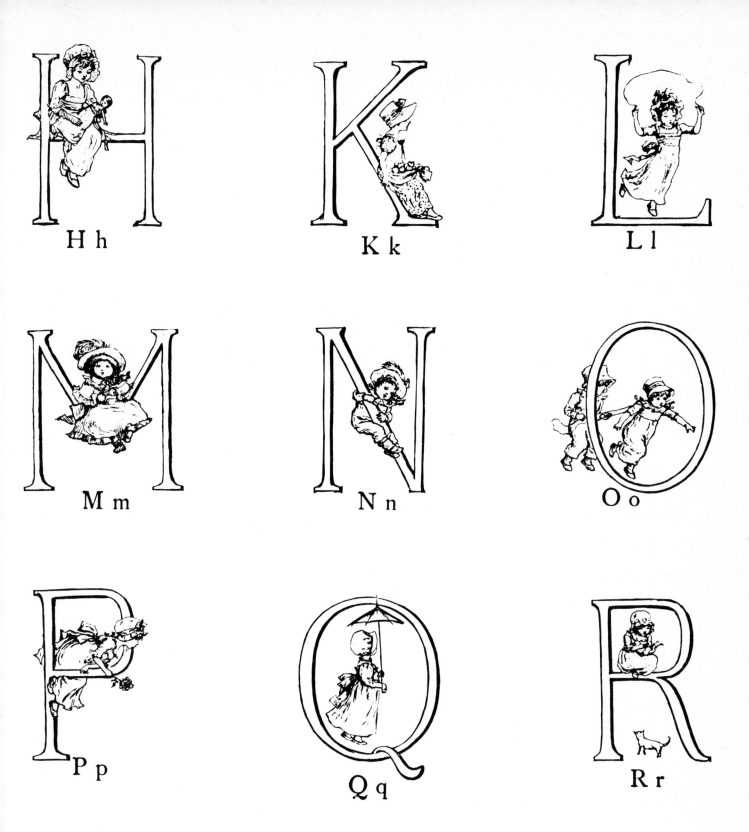

H h

K k

L l

M m

N n

O o

P p

Q q

R r

Illustrations from **The English Spelling-Book**
1884 (7 x 4½ ins)

The engraved illustrations printed in brown with text written by William Mavor were designed to teach spelling. Edmund Evans originally proposed that the book should be a collaboration between Randolph Caldecott and Kate Greenaway, but she flatly refused.

Frontispiece. **Marigold Garden.** 1885 (10¾ x 8½ ins)

Marigold Garden, 1885

Kate Greenaway wrote the verses for this book which was printed in an English edition of 6,500. The success of the illustrations was based on delicate inked lines and subtle washes. Caldecott offered helpful technical advice in 1878: 'The brown ink of which I discoursed will not, when thickly used with a pen, keep itself entirely together under the overwhelming influence of a brush with watercolour. . . But the liquid Indian ink used for lines will stand any number of damp assaults. This I know from experience. Believe me.'

Four Princesses (above)
Galley proof (10¾ x 8½ ins)
(Kate Greenaway Collection Hampstead)

Street Show (top left)
Watercolour, pen, brown ink, pencil (6½ x 7¾ ins)
(Clark Institute, Williamstown, Mass.)

When we went out with Grandmama (left)
Watercolour (5¼ x 5¼ ins)
(Port Sunlight)

Colour Plates

page 25
Bubbles
1887 (5 x 4 ins)
(Victoria and Albert Museum)

Colour engraving by Edmund Evans from six wood blocks for *Rhymes for the Young Folk* by William Allingham.

opposite
Frontispiece
The Pied Piper of Hamelin
1888 (9¾ x 8¾ ins)

Engraved and printed by Edmund Evans

Wishes (page 28)
(10¾ x 8½ ins)

The Cats have come to Tea (page 29)
(10¾ x 8½ ins)

WISHES.

OH, if you were a little boy,
  And I was a little girl—
Why you would have some whiskers grow,
  And then my hair would curl.

Ah! if I could have whiskers grow,
  I'd let you have my curls:
But what's the use of wishing it—
  Boys never can be girls.

THE CATS HAVE COME TO TEA.

A Apple Pie
1886 (8¼ x 10¼ ins)

Ruskin severely criticised this book: 'I am considerably vexed about *Apple Pie*. I really think you ought seriously to consult me before determining on the lettering of things so important. The titles are simple bill-sticking of the vulgarest sort, over the drawings—nor is there one of those that has the least melodious charm as a colour design—while the feet—from merely hopeless are becoming literal paddles or flappers. . .'

At last the people in a body
To the Town Hall came flocking:
"'Tis clear," cried they, "our Mayor's a noddy;
"And as for our Corporation—shocking

The Pied Piper of Hamelin
1888 (9¾ x 8¾ ins)

The 35 illustrations for this book are among her finest. Although she became confused with the German pseudo-mediaevalism, the costumes and settings brought the Pre-Raphaelite spirit into the nursery.

"Consult with carpenters and builders,
"And leave in our town not even a trace
"Of the rats!"—when suddenly, up the face
Of the Piper perked in the market-place,
With a, "First, if you please, my thousand guilders!"

The Pied Piper of Hamelin
1888 (9¾ x 8¾ ins)

Cover to **Kate Greenaway's Book of Games**
1889 (9 x 7¼ ins)

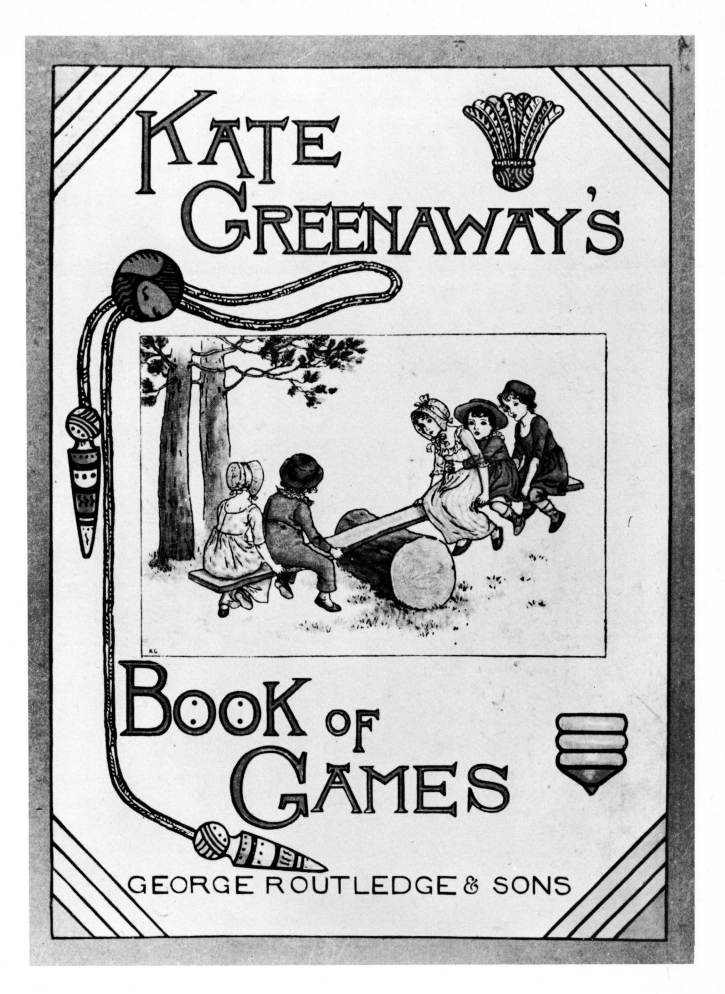

TOPS.

TOPS are common enough objects to most people, but there is some skill required in spinning them. There are also many different games. For "Peg in the Ring" (played with a peg top), draw a circle about three feet in diameter. One player begins by throwing his top into the centre, and whilst it is spinning the other players peg their tops at it, but if it

Kate Greenaway's Book of Games
1889 (9 x 7¼ ins)

Almanack for 1890
(3½ x 3 ins)

The black background and crimson and
yellow figures of the original make this
one of the most striking of the
Almanacks. She wrote on the night
theme: 'I have often wished lately to
paint a picture of night—it looks so
beautiful out of my window—the stars in
the sky. I think I shall do a little angel
rushing along in it, I want to do it as a
background to something.'

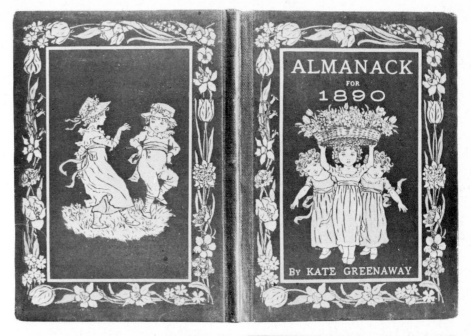

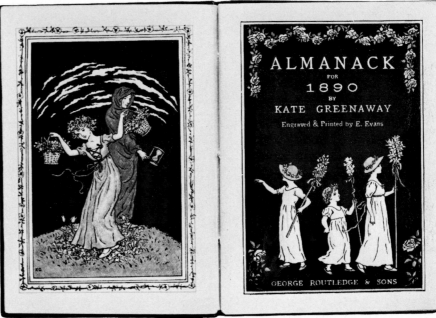

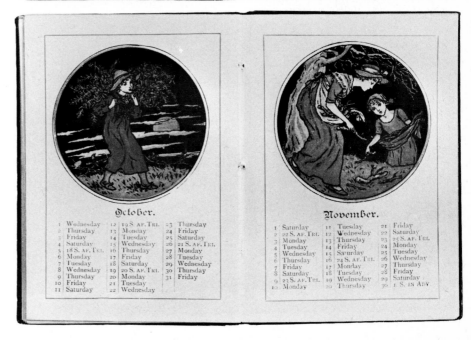

Collection of **Almanacks** illustrated by Kate Greenaway, 1883-1897 (excluding 1896) (Photograph: Courtesy Witt Library, London)

Little Miss Muffet
The April Baby's Book of Tunes
1900 (7¼ x 7½ ins)

Curiously, Kate Greenaway didn't believe in organised religions, but had a private conviction of goodness and beauty. She wrote in 1896: 'It feels to me so strange beyond anything I can think, to be able to believe in *any* of the known religions. Yet how beautiful if you could. Fancy feeling yourself saved, as they say—set apart to have a great reward.'

ONE WET DAY IN SPRINGTIME
We went out together,
And told all our secrets,
Nor thought of the weather.
THUS, love, in life's journey
O lean on my arm:
And let my affection
Protect you from harm.

Calendar of the Seasons *(above)*
1876 (5 x 3¾ ins)
(Victoria and Albert Museum)

Issued by Marcus Ward in two sheets, folded and stitched, with four pages of text.

Valentine *(left)*
c. 1875 (6½ x 5 ins)
(Kate Greenaway Collection—Hampstead)

Kate Greenaway's first Valentine, published by Marcus Ward in gold and colours, sold nearly 25,000 copies in a few weeks. Fairies and small children were the most usual themes. She regarded children as 'earthly angels to keep us from the stars'.

KATE GREENAWAY'S   CALENDAR FOR 1884

40

OOR little maid,
quite vexed indeed,
She stops to speak,
he pays no heed;

Yet seems she fair
and winning too;
Ah friend – the blame
must lie with you!

My CHRISTMAS greeting, love & kiss
To you he bears, then tell me this:-
What must he look in you to find
Who leaves so sweet a maid behind?

MARCUS WARD & CO

Greeting Card
(3¾ x 5 ins)
(Victoria and Albert Museum)

This card, from a series of three, shows the influence of Kate Greenaway's studies of illuminated manuscripts in the British Museum. The verse is similar in theme to her own unpublished sonnets.

Calendar for 1884 *(left)*
(26 x 18 ins)
(Victoria and Albert Museum)

Greeting Card
c. 1878 (6¼ x 4 ins)
(Victoria and Albert Museum)

From a series published by Marcus Ward

Colour Plates

opposite
The Peacock Girl
Watercolour
(Whereabouts unknown)

page 44
Robin Hood and the Blackbird, A Tale of a Christmas Feast
1878 (3½ x 5 ins)
(Victoria and Albert Museum)

Six Christmas cards, published in folio by Marcus Ward.

FATE SEND YOU FATTER GAME THAN THIS

A STEADY AIM AND NE'ER A MISS

A MERRY CHRISTMAS

IF E'ER YOU MAKE A LUCKY HIT

BE SURE YOU MAKE THE BEST OF IT

A HAPPY NEW YEAR

HEALTH & GOOD CHEER

A HAPPY CHRISTMAS

WHAT MATTER THO' THE FEAST BE SMALL

THE HEARTIER WELCOME GIVE TO ALL

FAR BEST OF ALL THE CHRISTMAS FUN

THE MERRY DANCE WHEN DINNER'S DONE

1.

A RHYME, a rhyme, a Christmas rhyme
Of what befell, at Christmas time,
To that bold hunter Robin Hood,
Maid Marian, and the archers good.
One year, whose date I don't remember,
It froze and snowed all thro' December;
Birds small and great died off in pairs;
The famished foxes ate the hares;
Deer were devoured by wolves and bears.
Said Robin to his merry men,
"No game is left." Said Marian then,
"For Christmas feast, some there must be,
Remember, you're invited me!"
So Robin donned his green and feather,
And the merry troop set forth together;
But nothing found all day, till, lo!
A poor starved blackbird cross'd the snow.
Bold Robin stopped and bent his bow;
Then Marian cried, "Forbear this time!"
But Robin shot—so runs the rhyme.

2.

A RHYME, a rhyme, a merry rhyme
Of what befell, at Christmas time,
To Robin Hood, his archers good,
And Marian, in merry Sherwood.
What Robin shot, they all averred,
Was scarcely worth the name of bird.
"And I shall always say 'twas mean
To kill a thing so poor and lean,"
Said Marian, the forest queen.
Said Allan-a-dale to Little John,
"Just look what we're to feast upon."
Cried Tuck the Friar, "My cooking, friends,
For all ill-luck shall make amends.
Said Robin Hood, "I did my best;
To thee, friend Friar, I leave the rest,"
"Then follow me, and you shall see,"
Said Tuck, "how soon a feast shall be
Prepared for this gay company,"
So after Tuck, in merry time,
They piped and marched—so runs the rhyme.

66
63

ROBIN HOOD & THE BLACKBIRD

A TALE OF A CHRISTMAS DINNER

MARCUS WARD & CO.
LONDON & BELFAST

Series of Christmas and New Year Cards
(4 x 4 ins) *(top only)*
(Kate Greenaway Collection Hampstead)

Card designs were often re-used in different formats, indicating the adaptability
of her designs.

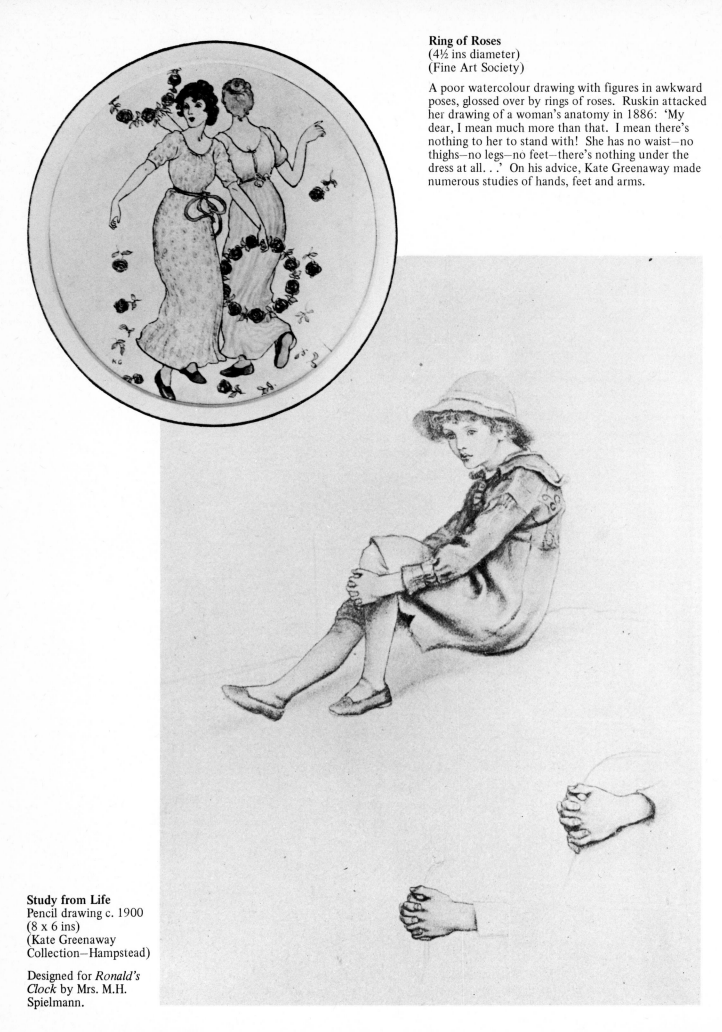

Ring of Roses
(4½ ins diameter)
(Fine Art Society)

A poor watercolour drawing with figures in awkward poses, glossed over by rings of roses. Ruskin attacked her drawing of a woman's anatomy in 1886: 'My dear, I mean much more than that. I mean there's nothing to her to stand with! She has no waist—no thighs—no legs—no feet—there's nothing under the dress at all. . .' On his advice, Kate Greenaway made numerous studies of hands, feet and arms.

Study from Life
Pencil drawing c. 1900
(8 x 6 ins)
(Kate Greenaway
Collection—Hampstead)

Designed for *Ronald's Clock* by Mrs. M.H. Spielmann.

The Elf Ring
Watercolour (7 x 5 ins)
(Whereabouts unknown)

Boy and Girl with a Cat
Watercolour (9¾ x 7½ ins)
(Port Sunlight)

These curious figures are posed in a suspended awkwardness—the seemingly weightless
basket is effortlessly balancing on the boy's head. The technical aspects of painting
fascinated Kate Greenaway. In 1895 she wrote: '. . . I seem to want to put in shade so
much more than I used to. I have got (sic) to love the making out of form by shade—the
softness of it. I love things soft and beautiful—not angular and hard as it is the fashion
to like them now.'

A Figure Study
Watercolour, bodycolour, pencil (16¼ x 11¾ ins)
(Laing Art Gallery, Newcastle)

A Pretty Christmas Visitor: When Grandmother was Young
Watercolour (7 x 5 ins)
(Photograph courtesy Witt Library, London)

The Flower Girl
Watercolour (22 x 17 ins)   (Photograph courtesy Witt Library, London)

The picture was probably painted in Islington (not later than 1877) using a favourite model who sold watercress; she was first painted in 1868 at the age of 8.

Ready for the Party
Watercolour (7¾ x 5¾ ins)
(Port Sunlight)

Kate Greenaway wrote to Ruskin in 1899: 'I'm not doing drawing that at all interests me now. They are just single figures of children which I always spoil by the backgrounds. I never can put a background into a painting of a single figure, while in a drawing there isn't the least difficulty. Perhaps I don't trouble about the reality in the drawing. I put things just where I want them, not, possibly, as they ought to do. And this seems to me the difficulty of full-length portraits. . . The most modern way is to have a highly done-out background and a figure lost in mist, but I don't see this.'

Grandmama's School Days *(right)*
(30 x 14 ins)
(Kate Greenaway Collection—Hampstead)

Mezzotint engraving by T.L. Atkinson, published by Thomas MacLean in 1881 in a declared edition to the Printsellers Association of 625.

THE ILLUSTRATED
LONDON NEWS

REGISTERED AT THE GENERAL POST-OFFICE FOR TRANSMISSION ABROAD.

No. 2021.—VOL. LXXII.　　　SATURDAY, MARCH 23, 1878.　　WITH TWO SUPPLEMENTS | SIXPENCE. By Post, 6½D.

"DARBY AND JOAN." BY KATE GREENAWAY.
IN THE EXHIBITION AT THE DUDLEY GALLERY.

preceding pages

Darby and Joan *(left)*
(12 x 9 ins)

Engraving from the painting exhibited at the Dudley Gallery in 1878 for *The Illustrated London News,* 23rd March 1878

A Christmas Dream *(right)*
(12 x 9 ins)

Engraving for *The Illustrated London News,*
26th December 1874

Croquet on the Lawn *(top)*
Pencil drawing (15 x 8 ins)
(Whereabouts unknown)

Lawn Tea *(above)*
Pencil drawing (15 x 8 ins)
(Whereabouts unknown)

Fairy Tale Grinaway Xmas Cards *(opposite)*
(10 x 6 ins)

Engraved illustration for *Punch,* 24th December 1881

MR. PUNCH'S "MOTHER HUBBARD" FAIRY TALE GRINAWAY CHRISTMAS CARDS.—(Second Series.)

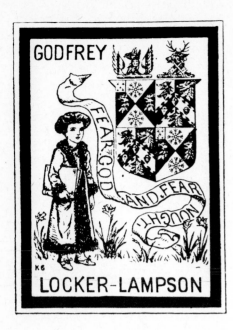  

Book Plates
(3 x 2 ins)
(Kate Greenaway Collection—Hampstead)

These were designed by Kate Greenaway for Frederick Locker Lampson and his family.

Reward Cards
(2 x 1½ ins)
(Kate Greenaway Collection—Hampstead)

The cards, based on designs from Kate Greenaway's books, were often found in Sunday schools marking the Bible passages of the deserving students.

Broadsheet Advertisement
From *The Illustrated London News,* 1879 (3 x 5 ins)

By 1877 Kate Greenaway was given regular commissions from this magazine. Her works appeared engraved on the covers and illustrating numerous articles.

Copybook Pages *(above)*
Pen and ink drawings by Thomas Gardner (1838-1891) (16 x 12 ins)
(Victoria and Albert Museum)

Following the publication of *Under the Window,* many similar copybooks were
created to aid craftsmen in adapting Kate Greenaway's designs for household
utensils, porcelain tea sets, dolls, children's clothing and wallpaper.

❧APPENDIX❧

The following list of works illustrated by Kate Greenaway was compiled from the British Museum catalogue, the catalogue of the Kate Greenaway Collection Hampstead, the catalogue of prints and drawings in the Victoria and Albert Museum London, from numerous collections in provincial galleries and museums, and London sale catalogues. The British Museum catalogue was used as the final authority in cases of discrepancy of dates.

Books

1867

INFANT AMUSEMENTS, OR HOW TO MAKE A NURSERY HAPPY by William H.G. Kingston with a frontispiece in black and white by Kate Greenaway, London: Griffith and Farran. (This is a little known work, the earliest book she illustrated)

1870

AUNT LOUISA'S NURSERY FAVOURITE: DIAMONDS AND TOADS from a series of London Toybooks with six unsigned colour illustrations by Kate Greenaway from water-colour drawings, London: Frederick Warne and Company

1871

MY SCHOOL DAYS IN PARIS by Margaret S. Jeune with illustrations by Kate Greenaway, London: Griffith and Farran

c. 1871

MADAME D'AULNOY'S FAIRY TALES: 1) THE FAIR ONE WITH GOLDEN LOCKS; 2) THE BABES IN THE WOOD; 3) TOM THUMB; 4) BLUEBEARD; 5) PUSS IN BOOTS; 6) THE BLUE BIRD; 7) THE WHITE CAT; 8) HOP O' MY THUMB; 9) RED RIDING HOOD, issued separately and illustrated from watercolour drawings by Kate Greenaway, Edinburgh: Gall and Inglis

1874

THE CHILDREN OF THE PARSONAGE by Aunt Cae with illustrations by Kate Greenaway, London: Griffith and Farran (second edition issued in 1875)

1875

FAIRY GIFTS; OR A WALLET OF WONDERS by Kathleen Knox with four full-page illustrations and seven small woodcuts by Kate Greenaway, engraved by John Greenaway, London: Griffith and Farran; New York: E.P. Dutton and Company (re-issued in 1882 and 1884)

THE FAIRY SPINNER by Miranda Hill with four black and white illustrations, colour title page and frontispiece by Kate Greenaway London: Marcus Ward and Company (new edition 1885)

A CRUISE IN THE ACORN by Alice Jerrold with six mounted illustrations in colour and gold also issued as greeting cards, London: Marcus Ward and Company

A CALENDAR OF THE SEASONS FOR 1876 with four illustrations by Kate Greenaway in colours and gold, London: Marcus Ward and Company (the illustrations were later used in FLOWERS AND FANCIES, 1883)

TURNASIDE COTTAGE by Mary Senior Clark with coloured frontispiece and title page and four full-page black and white illustrations by Kate Greenaway, London: Marcus Ward and Company

c. 1875

MELCOMB MANOR: A FAMILY CHRONICLE by Frederick Scarlett Potter with six full-page illustrations in colour and gold by Kate Greenaway, London: Marcus Ward and Company

CHILDREN'S SONGS with pictures and music, plates in colour and sepia, London: Marcus Ward and Company

1876

A CALENDAR OF THE SEASONS FOR 1877 with four illustrations by Kate Greenaway, London: Marcus Ward and Company

1877

TOM SEVEN YEARS OLD by H. Rutherford Russell with four full-page black and white illustrations by Kate Greenaway, London: Marcus Ward and Company

THE QUIVER OF LOVE: A COLLECTION OF VALENTINES ANCIENT AND MODERN with plates by Walter Crane and four full-page illustrations in colour and gold by Kate Greenaway including the frontispiece *Do I love you?*, *Surprise* and *Disdain;* a revised edition in 1880 contained different plates, London: Marcus Ward and Company (an additional revised edition FLOWERS AND FANCIES was issued in 1883) (cf. 1883 entry)

SEVEN BIRTHDAYS or THE CHILDREN OF FORTUNE, A FAIRY CHRONICLE by Kathleen Knox with illustrations by Kate Greenaway, London: Griffith and Farran

STARLIGHT STORIES TOLD TO BRIGHT EYES AND LISTENING EARS by Fanny Lablache with four full-page black and white illustrations by Kate Greenaway, London: Griffith and Farran

1878

POOR NELLY by Mrs Bonavia Hunt with numerous illustrations by Kate Greenaway, London: Cassell, Petter, Gilpin (the story was serialized in *Little Folks* in 1877)

TOPO: A TALE ABOUT ENGLISH CHILDREN IN ITALY by G.E. Brunefille with 44 black and white illustrations by Kate Greenaway, London: Marcus Ward and Company (second edition in 1880)

UNDER THE WINDOW with coloured pictures and rhymes for children by Kate Greenaway, engraved and printed by Edmund Evans, London: George Routledge; UNDER THE WINDOW: Pictures and Rhymes for Children after Kate Greenaway, New York: McLoughlin Bros (undated American edition); AM FENSTER: In Bildern und Versen von Kate Greenaway, der Deutsche text von Kathe Freiligrath-Kroeker, Munchen: Theodor Stroefer (1880 German edition) LA LANTERNE MAGIQUE par J. Levoisin avec les dessins de Kate Greenaway, Paris: Librairie Hachette et Cie (undated French edition). Both the German and French editions were engraved and printed by Edmund Evans

1879

THE HEIR OF REDCLYFFE by Charlotte M. Yonge with four full-page black and white illustrations by Kate Greenaway, London: Macmillan and Company (another edition in 1901)

HEARTSEASE; OR THE BROTHER'S WIFE by Charlotte M. Yonge with three full-page black and white illustrations by Kate Greenaway, London: Macmillan and Company (another edition in 1901)

AMATEUR THEATRICALS by Walter Herries Pollock with three illustrations by Kate Greenaway including a frontispiece *Comedy* and tailpiece *Going On*, London: Macmillan and Company (from the *Art at Home* series)

CALENDAR OF THE SEASONS FOR 1881 with four illustrations by Kate Greenaway, London: Marcus Ward and Company

c. 1880

THE OLD FARM GATE Stories in Prose and Verse for Little People with 25 full-page illustrations by Kate Greenaway, M.E. Edwards and Miriam Kerns, London: George Routledge

1881

THE LIBRARY by Andrew Lang; Austin Dobson wrote a chapter on modern English illustrated books including illustrations by Kate Greenaway, London: Macmillan and Company

LONDON LYRICS by Frederick Locker, a book of poems, with a frontispiece by Randolph Caldecott and tailpiece *Little Dinky* by Kate Greenaway, London (the American edition 1886 New York: White, Stokes and Allen, included Kate Greenaway's book plate printed in red on the title page)

A DAY IN A CHILD'S LIFE with music by Myles Foster and colour illustrations by Kate Greenaway, engraved and printed by Edmund Evans, London: George Routledge

MOTHER GOOSE OR THE OLD NURSERY RHYMES with illustrations by Kate Greenaway engraved and printed by Edmund Evans, London: George Routledge
SCÈNES FAMILIÈRES avec colour dessins de Kate Greenaway, Paris: Hachette (undated French edition of MOTHER GOOSE)

1882

THE ILLUSTRATED CHILDREN'S BIRTHDAY BOOK written in part and edited by F.E. Weatherly with illustrations, with 12 plates in colour, by Kate Greenaway and others, London: W.Mack

1882-3

LITTLE ANN AND OTHER POEMS by Jane and Ann Taylor, illustrated by Kate Greenaway, printed in colours by Edmund Evans in 1881, published London: George Routledge in 1883

POEMES INFANTINS PAR JANE ET ANN TAYLOR, traduction libre de J. Girardin, Paris: Hachette, 1883 (French edition)

1883

ALMANACK FOR 1883, four versions illustrated by Kate Greenaway, London: George Routledge

A CALENDAR OF THE MONTHS 1884, 12 colour illustrations by Kate Greenaway, London: Marcus Ward and Company

FLOWERS AND FANCIES, VALENTINES ANCIENT AND MODERN by B. Montgomerie

TROT'S JOURNEY pictures, rhymes and stories with over sixty woodcut illustrations by Kate Greenaway, New York: R. Worthington (originally published in *Little Folks* in Jan 1879)

TOYLAND, TROT'S JOURNEY, AND OTHER POEMS AND STORIES with illustrations by Kate Greenaway, New York: R. Worthington (another undated edition)

THE 'LITTLE FOLKS' PAINTING BOOK with a series of 107 outline engravings for watercolour painting by Kate Greenaway with verses and stories by George Weatherly, London: Cassell, Petter, Gilpin

c. 1879

THE 'LITTLE FOLKS' NATURE PAINTING BOOK with the headpiece and a few figures by Kate Greenaway with stories and verses by by George Weatherly, London: Cassell, Petter, Gilpin

A FAVOURITE ALBUM OF FUN AND FANCY with four illustrations by Kate Greenaway to the allegory *Kribs and the Wonderful Bird*, London: Cassell, Petter, Gilpin

THREE BROWN BOYS AND OTHER HAPPY CHILDREN by Ellen Haile with illustrations by Kate Greenaway and others, New York: Cassell and Company

THE TWO GRAY GIRLS AND THEIR OPPOSITE NEIGHBOURS by Ellen Haile with black and white illustrations by Kate Greenaway, M.E. Edwards and others, New York: Cassell and Company

1880

KATE GREENAWAY'S BIRTHDAY BOOK FOR CHILDREN with 382 illustrations, 12 plates in colour, printed by Edmund Evans, London: George Routledge;
LES PETITE LIVRE DES SOUVENIRS, Paris: Hachette (undated French edition)
KATE GREENAWAY'S GEBURTSTAG-BUCH FÜR KINDER, mit 382 illustrationen gezeichnet von Kate Greenaway, Munchen: Theodor Stroefer (undated German edition)

FREDDIE'S LETTER: STORIES FOR LITTLE PEOPLE with a frontispiece by Kate Greenaway, and designs by other illustrators, London: George Routledge

Ranking and Thomas K. Tully, with four full page colour illustrations by Kate Greenaway, London: Marcus Ward and Company (a revised edition of THE QUIVER OF LOVE, 1876)

TALES FROM THE EDDA by Helen Zimmern with two full-page illustrations by Kate Greenaway (although her name is incorrectly affixed to illustration on p 126) and others, London: W. Swan Sonnenschein and Company

1883-4

FORS CLAVIGERA by John Ruskin: Letters to the Workmen and Labourers of Great Britain: Letter the 91st Sept 1883 with one illustration; Letter the 93rd Christmas 1883 with one illustration; and Letter the 94th March 1884 with two illustrations, all by Kate Greenaway, London and Orpington: George Allen

1884

ALMANACK FOR 1884 illustrated by Kate Greenaway and printed by Edmund Evans, London: George Routledge (this edition marked a new enlarged format)

A PAINTING BOOK by Kate Greenaway with outline engravings from her various works, several in sepia, London: George Routledge

LANGUAGE OF FLOWERS illustrated by Kate Greenaway, printed in colours by Edmund Evans, London: George Routledge

SONGS FOR THE NURSERY: A Collection of Children's Poems edited by Robert Ellice Mack with black and white illustrations by Kate Greenaway and others, London: W. Mack

c. 1884

KATE GREENAWAY'S CAROLS issued as four pictorial cards with coloured figures, borders and music, London: George Routledge

1885

THE ENGLISH SPELLING-BOOK by William Mavor illustrated by Kate Greenaway, engraved and printed by Edmund Evans, London: George Routledge

London: Cassell and Company (the advertisements are dated 1886)

1887

ALMANACK FOR 1887 illustrated by Kate Greenaway, London: George Routledge

QUEEN VICTORIA'S JUBILEE GARLAND with four full-page illustrations by Kate Greenaway, three of which are in colour, printed by Edmund Evans, London: George Routledge (this was a booklet comprised of previously published illustrations)

1888

ORIENT LINE GUIDE Chapters for Travellers by Sea and Land edited by W.J. Loftie with half-title drawing and 14 outline drawings of dainty children carrying flowers and fruit by Kate Greenaway, London: Sampson, Low, Marston, Searle and Rivington (her designs seemed inappropriate in such a publication, however, W.J. Loftie was her first publisher)

ALMANACK FOR 1888 illustrated by Kate Greenaway, London: George Routledge

THE PIED PIPER OF HAMELIN by Robert Browning with 35 colour illustrations by Kate Greenaway, engraved and printed by Edmund Evans, London: George Routledge (the rare first edition was marked *Glasgow* although G. Routledge maintained offices there only a short time)

AROUND THE HOUSE Stories and Poems with black and white, sepia illustrations by Kate Greenaway taken from *Little Folks, The Illustrated London News* etc., New York: Worthington and Company

1889

ALMANACK FOR 1889 illustrated by Kate Greenaway, London: George Routledge (the designs were borrowed from the letters of KATE GREENAWAY'S ALPHABET, 1885)

KATE GREENAWAY'S BOOK OF GAMES with 24 full-page colour illustrations by Kate Greenaway, engraved and printed by Edmund Evans, London: George Routledge

THE ROYAL PROGRESS OF KING PEPITO by Beatrice F. Cresswell illustrated by Kate Greenaway, engraved and printed by Edmund Evans, London: The Society for Promoting Christian Knowledge

1890

ALMANACK FOR 1890 with illustrations by Kate Greenaway, engraved and printed by Edmund Evans, London: George Routledge

1891

KATE GREENAWAY'S ALMANACK FOR 1891 with illustrations by Kate Greenaway, London: George Routledge

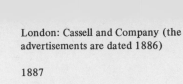

ALMANACK FOR 1885 illustrated by Kate Greenaway, London: George Routledge

DAME WIGGINS OF LEE AND HER SEVEN WONDERFUL CATS by a lady of ninety, with four additional verses by John Ruskin and four new illustrations by Kate Greenaway, London and Orpington: George Allen (a sixth edition was published in 1913)

MARIGOLD GARDEN with pictures and rhymes by Kate Greenaway, printed in colour by Edmund Evans, London: George Routledge

c. 1885

KATE GREENAWAY'S ALPHABET with each letter a coloured illustration by Kate Greenaway, London: George Routledge (a re-issue of the individual letters in THE ENGLISH SPELLING-BOOK, 1885)

KATE GREENAWAY'S ALBUM with 192 coloured illustrations with gold borders, printed by Edmund Evans, London: George Routledge (one of the rarest Greenaway books: only eight copies were printed, the book never being published)

1886

ALMANACK FOR 1886 illustrated by Kate Greenaway, London: George Routledge

A APPLE PIE with illustrations by Kate Greenaway, engraved and printed by Edmund Evans, London: George Routledge (originally one of AUNT LOUISA'S TOYBOOKS No 2 1868, London: Frederick Warne)

THE QUEEN OF THE PIRATE ISLE by Bret Harte illustrated by Kate Greenaway, engraved and printed by Edmund Evans, London: Chatto and Windus. Only a few copies were sent for the American edition, Boston and New York: Houghton Mifflin and Company 1887

BABY'S BIRTHDAY BOOK with coloured illustrations by Kate Greenaway and others, London: Marcus Ward and Company

c. 1886

RHYMES FOR THE YOUNG FOLK by William Allingham with illustrations by Kate Greenaway and others, engraved and printed in colour and sepia by Edmund Evans,

1892

KATE GREENAWAY'S ALMANACK FOR 1892 with illustrations by Kate Greenaway, London: George Routledge

1893

KATE GREENAWAY'S ALMANACK FOR 1893 with illustrations by Kate Greenaway, London: George Routledge

1894

KATE GREENAWAY'S ALMANACK FOR 1894 with illustrations by Kate Greenaway from THE ENGLISH SPELLING-BOOK, 1885, London: George Routledge

1895

KATE GREENAWAY'S ALMANACK FOR 1895 with illustrations by Kate Greenaway London: George Routledge

1896

KATE GREENAWAY'S CALENDAR FOR 1897 with coloured figures of childhood, youth, and old age, London: George Routledge (the illustrations are similar to those of KATE GREENAWAY'S CAROLS c. 1884)

1897

KATE GREENAWAY'S ALMANACK AND DIARY FOR 1897, London: J.M. Dent and Company

1898

KATE GREENAWAY'S CALENDAR FOR 1899, London: George Routledge

1900

THE APRIL BABY'S BOOK OF TUNES WITH THE STORY OF HOW THEY CAME TO BE WRITTEN by Countess von Arnim illustrated with 16 colour-lithographed plates, six full-page, by Kate Greenaway, London: Macmillan (also an American edition, New York: Macmillan, 1900) (the first use of colour-lithography rather than Evan's wood-engravings)

1901

LONDON AFTERNOONS by W.J. Loftie with a drawing from one of the Cottonian Manuscripts for the Society for the Promotion of Christian Knowledge depicting an effigy of Abbot John of Berkhamstead by Kate Greenaway, London: Cassell and Company

Books issued posthumously:

1903

LITTLEDOM CASTLE AND OTHER TALES by Mrs M.H. Spielmann illustrated by Arthur Rackham, Hugh Thomson, Harry Furniss, Kate Greenaway and others, London: George Routledge (Kate Greenaway made two drawings to *Ronald's Clock*)

1908

DE LIBRIS Prose and Verse by Austin Dobson with illustrations by Kate Greenaway, Hugh Thomson and others, London: Macmillan (second edition 1911)

1920

PICTURES FOR PAINTING by Kate Greenaway with outlines from her various works, London and New York: Frederick Warne and Company

KATE GREENAWAY'S ALMANACKS FOR 1924, 1925, 1926, 1928 and 1929

Periodicals

THE PEOPLE'S MAGAZINE 1 Jan 1873 with an illustration to the poem *Nonsense about Cat's-Cradle* on the newly instigated *Children's Page* p 24; 1 Feb 1873 illustration to the story *Bebel* p 97; 1 July 1873 illustration to the story *Ida of the Nut-Bush* p 24; 1 Oct 1873 illustration to the story *Thinking in the Garden* p 225; 1 Nov 1873 illustration to the story *Ness Owen* p 305

CASSELL'S MAGAZINE New Series, London Vol 9 1874 with a woodcut drawing *Look Downard on the Wave* to the story *Babette* engraved by John Greenaway p 225

THE ILLUSTRATED LONDON NEWS Vol 54 26 Dec 1874 with full-page engraving *A Christmas Dream* p 605; 15 Dec 1875 a full page engraving *Dolly's Dream* p 28

LITTLE FOLKS New and Enlarged Series, Cassell and Company, London Vol 3 July 1876 a full-page engraving *Primroses* p 220; five small drawings to the verse story *The Birdie's Warning* p 344-5; Vol 4 Dec 1876 six small drawings to the verse story *Toyland* pp 71-3; five small drawings to the verse story *Chatterbox Hall* pp 199-201; a small drawing to the serial *Things learnt without lessons...* p 153; a small drawing of the letter *C* p 263; a small drawing *Little Knots of Boys* p 408; Vol 5 July 1877 six small drawings to the verse story *Lily's Migration* pp 51-4; a small drawing *Jenny's Little Friend* p 58; a small drawing of a little boy and girl blowing a bubble for *Illustrations of Shakespeare—No 1: Trifles, light as air*; four small drawings to the story *The Raven's Riddle* pp 180-1; a small drawing of the letter *M* p 242; a small drawing of a girl and boy having tea illustrating the story *Bess and Tim* p 248; two small *Illustrations of Shakespeare: When shall we three meet again?* (depicting three girls dancing) and *Nature hath form'd strange fellows in her time* (depicting a curious flower pot dwarf) p 317; a small drawing of a girl with hoop illustrating the poem *Little Folks* p 349; five small drawings to the story *Put's Journey* pp 367-70; Vol 6 Dec 1877 four small drawings illustrating the serial story *Poor Nelly* pp 1, 5, 8, 9; seven drawings to the verse story *Bobby and Prissy* pp 24-6; a small drawing *Marjorie and the Brownie* p 92; a small drawing of the letter *M* to *Poor Nelly* Chapter V p 98; and two drawings pp 100-1; a half-page drawing to the song *A Rhyme of the Wind* p 122; a half-page illustration to the poem *The March of the Men of Brook* p 137; three small illustrations to *Poor Nelly* Chapter VI pp 161,165; a small drawing *Ready for Pudding* p 184; a small drawing of a girl feeding a parrot p 226; a small letter *O* and two drawings to the serial *Poor Nelly* pp 229, 233; a small drawing to the verse story *The Shepherd Boy's Little Sister* p 224; a half-page drawing to the song *A Song of Three Children* p 251; a small drawing of the letter *T* and three drawings to *Poor Nelly* pp 251, 264-5; a small drawing of a girl fishing p 313; a small drawing of the letter *I* and three small drawings to *Poor Nelly* pp 353, 357, 361; Vol 7 Jan 1878 a title page drawing of three children dancing (repeated from Vol 5 p 317); four small illustrations to the story *Maggie's Adventure* by Julia Goddard pp 56-57 (repeated in ST NICHOLAS Vol VI 1879 p 383); a small illustration *Folding her hands over her eyes* p 80; three small drawings to the story *The Golden Rose* by Julia Goddard pp 120-1; three small drawings to the verse story *Dolly: A Set of Songs* pp 176-8; a small drawing of the letter *I* and four small drawings to the serial story *Into the View* by Mrs A.H. Martin pp 240-1, 244-5; a small drawing of the letter *T* p 282; two small drawings of a father and his daughter pp 284-5; four small drawings to *The Story of Anna and Peter* pp 312-4; Vol 8 July a title page drawing of a boy and girl within a circle; a small drawing *The Tale of Ten Crows* p 93; a small drawing of the letter *W* and two drawings to the story *Minna's Wonderful Dream* pp 120-2; a small drawing of children

with a dead caged bird p 141; a small drawing to *An Illustrated Quotation— Amazed, the gazing rustics ranged around* (A group of children watching butterflies) p 179; a small drawing of the letter *W* and three drawings to *The Boy Who Was Too Fond of Play* pp 248-9; a small drawing of a boy and a pig illustrating the story *Left Behind* p 270; a half-page drawing *Fritz Hears the History of Bullerbasius* for *The Story of Bullerbasius* by M.K. Woods p 336; Vol 9 Jan 1879 a title page drawing of two boys within a circle; four small, one half-page drawing to the story *Hide-and-Seek in a Manor-house* pp 20-2; a Christmas Card and New Year Card designed for a French verse-translation competition, one depicting two girls with holly branches and wreath, the other a boy and girl in winter clothing p 41; three small drawings to the story *Trot's Journey* pp 107-8, 110; a small drawing of children painting to advertise *The Little Folks Painting Book* for 1879 with a £4 prize competition and specially created *Little Folks Fine Art Mount Colour Box*; two small drawings to the story *Blowing Bubbles and What Became of It*, one drawing of a girl on a flying carpet *Going to Fairyland* pp 247-249

HAPPY DAYS: THE LITTLE FOLKS ANNUAL FOR 1880 with a full-page frontispiece *Sisters*; two full-page calendar drawings Jan, Feb, July, Aug pp 4, 7; Vol 11 Jan 1880 a title page drawing of three girls playing in sand; four small drawings to the verse story *Kribs and the Wonderful Bird* pp 24-5; a half-page drawing to the poem *Slumber Song* p 80; a small drawing of children promenading with wheat to the poem *The Little Gleaners* p 112; a half-page drawing to the poem *The Child and the Cowslips* p 144 a small drawing to the poem *A Slice of the Moon* p 184; Vol 12 July 1880 a full-page drawing *The Stolen Apple* to the story *An Apple Story* by Julia Goddard (originally the cover for *The Illustrated London News* Christmas Number 1877 called *Little Loves*

THE GLAD TIME: LITTLE FOLKS ANNUAL FOR 1881 with a small drawing to the poem *A Song of the Seasons* by Julia Goddard p 41 (the title page claims 'with numerous illustrations by Kate Greenaway and others', its design by George Cruikshank borrows from her drawings of children)

THE ROUND ROBIN Annual to OLD MERRY'S MONTHLY edited by Old Merry with two full-page plates by Kate Greenaway

pp 287, 602, London: Frederick Warne undated (these plates reappeared in TALES FROM THE EDDA, 1883)

THE ILLUSTRATED LONDON NEWS Christmas Number 1877 with a cover *Little Loves* and full-page engraving *Three Home Rulers* p 4

ST NICHOLAS Scribner's Illustrated Magazine for Girls and Boys, New York Vol V Dec 1877 with a Christmas Card depicting a page boy p 91; Jan 1878 a New Year Card depicting a serving maiden p 122; Vol VI Jan 1879 with eight small drawings to the story *Children's Day at St Pauls* pp 148-52, 154-5; March 1879 with a small drawing to the poem *Calling the Flowers* p 333; April 1879 with four drawings to the story *Beating the Bounds* by Thomas Hughes including the half-page drawing *Ready for the March* p 392; two small drawings p 393; *The Beadle Leads the Procession* p 395 depicting a curious fat coachman; a small drawing to the poem *The Little Big Woman and the Big Little Girl* p 383 (the old woman similar in style to Dame Wiggins); Vol VII Feb 1880 with a small drawing of the letter *W*

ROUTLEDGE'S EVERY GIRL'S ANNUAL FOR 1879 with a coloured frontispiece and title page; FOR 1880 with coloured frontispiece, title page, black and white drawing *Children of the Week*; FOR 1881, FOR 1882 both with coloured frontispiece and title page

THE ILLUSTRATED LONDON NEWS 23 Mar 1878 with full-page engraving in black and white *Darby and Joan;* 15 Feb 1879 with full-colour frontispiece *St Valentine's Day* and three drawings from a set of seven; 27 Dec 1879 with a full-page engraving *A Juvenile Christmas Party* p 593; a Christmas Issue 1879 with a full-page engraving *Tired Out*

PUNCH Vol 79 4 Dec 1880 with a caricature of Kate Greenaway and other illustrators *Mr. Punch Surveys Children's Christmas Books* p 254; Vol 81 10 Dec 1881 with a full-page parody *Mother Hubbard* p 275; 17 Dec 1881 with a full-page parody *The Royal Birthday Book* p 279; 24 Dec 1881 with a full-page parody *Grinaway Xmas Cards* p 287

LITTLE WIDE AWAKE FOR 1880, George Routledge, London with a coloured frontis-

piece repeated on the cover and two woodcuts; FOR 1881 with coloured frontispiece repeated on the cover; FOR 1885 with coloured frontispiece; FOR 1888 and FOR 1889 both with coloured frontispiece

THE ILLUSTRATED LONDON NEWS Christmas Number 1881 with full-page engraving *Nelly's Dream* p 8; Christmas Number 1882 with full-page engraving *We Wish You a Merry Christmas* p 1

ROUTLEDGE'S CHRISTMAS NUMBER Christmas 1882 with full-page colour frontispiece *Little Fanny*

CENTURY MAGAZINE Feb 1883 with an article *Frederick Locker* with Kate Greenaway's tailpiece illustration from *London Lyrics* p 595

THE MAGAZINE OF ART Vol VI Jan 1883 with an article *Art in the Nursery* by Austin Dobson with four drawings by Kate Greenaway pp 127-32; May 1883 with a drawing illustrating Austin Dobson's poem *Home Beauty* p 277

THE ILLUSTRATED LONDON NEWS Christmas Number 1883 with a double page colour plate *'Tiss Me!*

SUNSHINE London Jan 1884 with two small black and white drawings illustrating *Children in Council* p 15

HARPER'S YOUNG PEOPLE Vol 1 20 Dec with an illustration to the printed music *A Christmas Carol* p 80

THE ILLUSTRATED LONDON NEWS Christmas Number 1885 a small drawing of a girl for an advertisement *DuBarry's Revalanta Food* for babies p 30

THE GIRL'S OWN PAPER London Vol VII Nov 1886 with a coloured plate *Afternoon Tea* and half-title drawings; Vol VIII Sept 1887 with frontispiece *Golden Summer* and title page; Vol XII Jan 1891 with frontispiece *Garland Day* printed in sepia; Vol XXIII Jan 1902 with coloured frontispiece, portrait and unpublished sketches with the colour plate *Afternoon Tea* laid in

THE GIRL'S OWN ANNUAL London for 1886-7 with colour frontispiece *Afternoon Tea* and title page; 1890-91 with colour frontispiece *Garland Day*; 1891-92 with coloured plate *Golden Summer*, some editions included the extra numbers *Love Light* and *Maidenhair*; 1901-2 with an article by Mary J. Evans on Kate Greenaway, with her portrait and hitherto unpublished drawings

THE CRITIC New York 8 Dec 1888 an account of *The Pied Piper* illustrated by Kate Greenaway

HOLLY LEAVES the Christmas Number of the Illustrated Sporting and Dramatic News London 1889 with full-page illustration

Preparing for Christmas by Kate Greenaway, engraved by John Greenaway

THE CHRISTMAS TREE London (undated c. 1890) with a full-page plate *Little Fanny*

THE ENGLISH ILLUSTRATED MAGAZINE London Christmas 1894 with a full-page coloured plate *A Sailor's Wife*; Christmas 1898 with a full-page plate *Primroses*

THE LADIES HOME JOURNAL Philadelphia Mar, April 1895 with drawings to Laura E. Richard's verse *April Children*; Christmas 1895 drawings to *Maidie's Dance* p 29; Mar 1896 drawings to *Off to Dancing School* p 15; May 1896 drawings to *In Springtime* p 13; Nov 1896 drawings to *The Picnic Tea* (These illustrations were reissued with the verses in a Supplement Edition)

Greeting Cards

Due to numerous editions and derivative designs, an accurate cataloguing of cards designed by Kate Greenaway is a difficult project. Gleeson White lists twelve sets, vaguely described but known to be by her (cf. *Studio* 1894); a number are catalogued in the Kate Greenaway Collection, Hampstead, and the Victoria and Albert Museum, including the following:

VALENTINES: *One Wet Day in Springtime* colour lithograph card, Marcus Ward c. 1875 (6½ x 4 ins); card depicting a boy and girl sitting in a blossom-laden twig, colour lithograph, Marcus Ward c. 1875 (5½ x 4 ins); *Do I Love You?*, *Surprise, Disdain* and others taken from *The Quiver of Love*, 1876, colour lithograph, Marcus Ward c. 1876 (8¾ x 7¼ ins); card depicting a boy and girl looking at a bird's nest, colour lithograph with paper lace, Marcus Ward c. 1876 (7½ x 5¾ ins); card depicting a boy and girl beneath an arch of roses, colour lithograph, Marcus Ward c. 1876 (7½ x 5¾ ins)

CHRISTMAS AND NEW YEAR CARDS: a set of four cards *The Youth of Sir Joshua's Day* with verses by E.K. and G.P. Meade depicting four children in fancy dress, colour lithographs from the series No.265, Marcus Ward c. 1875 (5¼ x 3½ ins); two Christmas cards depicting a page-boy carrying a hat, a girl holding a sealed letter with verses by Julia Goddard, colour lithographs, Marcus Ward c. 1875 (5¼ x 3½ ins); three Christmas cards

set of twelve text cards *Feed My Lambs*
colour lithograph, Marcus Ward n.d.
(3½ x 3 ins)

each depicting two children with verses by
G.P. Meade, colour lithographs, Marcus Ward
c. 1875 (3¾ x 5 ins horizontal); a set *Robin
Hood and the Blackbird—A Tale of a
Christmas Feast,* four cards with rhyming
verse, colour lithographs, Marcus Ward
c. 1878 (from a series of six designs published
as a booklet under the same title); the
Coachmen series of Christmas and New Year
cards, a set of three depicting a boy coachman;
a boy waving a handkerchief; a girl throwing
a kiss, colour lithographs, Marcus Ward
c. 1878 (6 x 4¼ ins) (two are illustrated in
Gleeson White's article); two Christmas cards
depicting six girls with a rose garland, colour
lithograph, Marcus Ward c. 1878 (6¼ x 3 ins);
a set of four New Year cards from the Kate
Greenaway Series No 501 *Happy Pair, Little
White Lamb, Golden Rod, Greeting to You*
with verse on reverse side, colour lithographs
with gold edges, Goodall n.d. (4½ x 3¼ ins);
a set of three Christmas cards to the Kate
Greenaway Series No 503 *Friendly Voices
Come from Far Away, I'd Like to Sit and
Sip my Tea, To Wish You a Merry Christmas*
(depicting three little misses) colour
lithographs, Goodall n.d. (3½ x 2¾ ins)
(later issued in a larger format series);
a series of Christmas and New Year cards *I
Come to Wish You a Merry Christmas, I
Come to Wish You a Happy New Year*
colour lithographs, Marcus Ward n.d.
(5¾ x 3 ins); a series of Christmas and New
Year cards *In a Dream I Saw Them Stand,
Poor Little Maid, Good Old Times* colour
lithographs, Marcus Ward n.d. (5 x 3¾ ins);
*With My Best Wishes, I Come to Wish You a
Happy New Year* colour lithographs, Marcus
Ward n.d. (6 x 5 ins); *May All the Seed Thou
Sowest Take Deep Hold* colour lithograph,
Marcus Ward (6 x 3½ ins); *May Christmas
Bring You Happiness* colour lithograph,
Marcus Ward n.d. (4 x 3 ins); *May Christmas
Bring You Store of Blisses* colour lithograph,
Marcus Ward n.d. (4¼ x 3 ins)

MISCELLANEOUS CARDS: a series of
cards *I Was Wishing I Could Bid You, Though
Today I Cannot Meet You, I'm Sure I Have
Not Forgotten* colour lithographs, Marcus
Ward n.d. (6 x 4¼ ins); *May The Year Bring
You Hours..., The Wind May Be Bleak...,*
colour lithographs, Marcus Ward n.d.
(7½ x 3¾ ins); Easter cards *Now Christ is
Risen from the Dead, Joy and Peace Be
Thine Today* colour lithographs, Marcus Ward
n.d. (7½ x 4¼ ins); birthday card *Sweet
Maidens Will Hear My Friend* colour
lithograph, Marcus Ward n.d. (3½ x 3 ins); a

Ephemera

HANDBILL–CHARITY CHILDREN a hand-
bill of psalms to be sung at the Anniversary of
the Charity Children 1877 with illustrations
drawn in the margin by Kate Greenaway

BROADSIDES–THE ILLUSTRATED
LONDON NEWS a series of colour illustrated
advertisements by Kate Greenaway including
the designs *Four Carol Singers; In Church; In
the Snow; Little Miss with Muff; Little Miss
with Fan; Young Partners* 1879

PROGRAMMES two Programmes for
Concert and Entertainment at the Concert
Hall, Blackheath 10 Dec and 11 Dec 1883
by Kate Greenaway, each with a different
coloured drawing of a child and flowers with
gold border (6 x 4¼ ins)

FINE ART ENGRAVING–GRANDMAMA'S
SCHOOL DAYS an engraving by Kate
Greenaway printed in colours (another edition
in black and white) engraved by Thomas Lewis
Atkinson published by Thos. MacLean, the
black and white edition declared to the
Printseller's Association 1 Nov 1881 in an
edition of 625

INVITATION to the Collection of Drawings
by Kate Greenaway and Hugh Thomson 7
Feb 1891, a small folder with colour
illustrated cover of a girl writing on a table
by Kate Greenaway

BOOKPLATES designs by Kate Greenaway
for Victoria Alexandrina May Cecil Herbert,
Frederick Locker, Dorothy Locker-Lampson,
Godfrey Locker-Lampson, Hannah Jane
Locker-Lampson, Maud Locker-Lampson,
Oliver Locker-Lampson (the Locker-Lampson
plates 1898) and Sarah Nickson

PATTERN BOOKS a copybook containing
line drawings from UNDER THE WINDOW
for silverware by Thomas Gardner, one dated
1883 (in the collection of the Victoria and
Albert Museum); a Catalogue of Patent
Transferring Papers by Briggs and Company
Manchester, n.d. with pp 86-91 containing
12 designs of village life after Kate Greenaway
drawings

PATCHWORK QUILT with embroidered
designs from Kate Greenaway's books 1885

Many other objects were produced with
designs from Greenaway books including
porcelain tea services, figurines, china,
silver jewelry, a large number of buttons, tiles,
glass vases and dolls complete with clothing,
wallpaper, trade cards advertising soaps,
baby food, etc.

Catalogues

FINE ART SOCIETY Exhibition No 83
Catalogue of a Collection of Drawings by Miss

Kate Greenaway and Hugh Thomson with a
prefatory note by Lionel Robinson, title
page and text illustrations by Kate Greenaway,
London 1891; Exhibition No 115 *Catalogue
of a Collection of Water-Colour Drawings by
Kate Greenaway R.I.* London 1894;
Exhibition No 175 *Catalogue of an
Exhibition of Water-Colour Drawings by
Kate Greenaway R.I.* London 1898; *Catalogue
of Water-Colour Drawings left by the late
Kate Greenaway* with prefatory note by
M.H. Spielmann, London 1902

*Beschrijvende Catalogus van Engelsche
Prentkunst voor groote en Kleine Kindern,
Walter Crane, Kate Greenaway, Randolph
Caldecott, Hugh Thomson etc.* Gravenhage
1893

ANDERSON GALLERIES *The Kate
Greenaway Collection of Miss M.I. Meacham*
New York 1921 (a very complete list of
books, articles, ephemera)

MAGGS BROTHERS LTD. *Catalogue of
Original Drawings by Kate Greenaway and
Hugh Thomson* London Nov 1938

PHILLIPS AUCTIONEERS *Water-Colours,
Drawings and Books by Kate Greenaway*
London 16 Nov 1971

Exhibitions

THE COLUMBIAN EXHIBITION, CHICAGO:
1893 Five drawings among those exhibited
were sold: Title page *Marigold Garden; The
Mulberry Bush; Girl Drawing a Chaise; Little
Girlie; Little Phyllis*

THE DUDLEY GALLERY: 1868 *Kilmeny—an
illustrated versified legend—a series of six
drawings of fairies on wood;* 1869 *The Fairies
of Caldon Low;* 1870 *Apple Blossom—A Spring
Idyll;* 1872 1) *A Study* 2) *A Reverie;* 1875
Little Miss Prim; 1876 *Little Girls as Play;*
1877 1) *In Spring Time* 2) *Dorothy* 3) *Birthday
Tea* 4) *A Procession of Children with Flowers;*
1878 1) *A Procession of Children* 2) *Darby and
Joan* 3) *Miss Patty;* 1879 1) *Prissy* 2) *A
Morning Call*

THE FINE ART SOCIETY, LONDON
1880 An exhibition of drawings from *Under
the Window*
1891 Exhibition No 83: 150 Drawings (her
first one-man show)
1894 Exhibition No 115: 120 Water-Colour
Drawings

1898 Exhibition No 175: 127 Water-Colour Drawings
1902 Posthumous Exhibition of 210 Water-Colour Drawings

PARIS EXHIBITION: 1889 A series of drawings

THE ROYAL ACADEMY: 1877 *Musing;* 1878 *Little Girl with Doll;* 1879 *Misses;* 1880 *Little Girl with Fan;* 1890 *Portrait of a Little Lad; A Girl's Head;* 1895 *Baby Boy*

THE ROYAL INSTITUTE OF PAINTERS IN WATERCOLOURS: (1889 elected a member) 1893 *A Girl* 1895 1) *Gleaners Going Home* 2) *Girl and Two Children* 3) *Little Girl in Red* 4) *Taking a Nosegay;* 1896 *Little Bo-Peep;* 1897 1) *Girl in Hat and Feathers* 2) *Two Little Girls in a Garden*

THE ROYAL MANCHESTER INSTITUTION 1873 *A Fern Gatherer*

ROYAL SOCIETY OF BRITISH ARTISTS: (SUFFOLK STREET GALLERIES) 1870 *A Peeper;* 1872/3 1) *Little Watercress Girl* 2) *Head of a German Girl;* 1873 1) *A Fern Gatherer* 2) Untitled watercolour with verse; 1873/4 1) *Little Miss* 2) *The Milk Maid* 3) *A Flower Girl;* 1875 *Buttercups;* 1875/6 1) *Apples* 2) *Little Walnut Girl*

MESSRS VAN BAERLE, GLASGOW:1892 Exhibition of 20 Water-Colour Drawings

Biographical Sources—Books

H.M. Cundall, **Kate Greenaway Pictures** from originals presented by her to John Ruskin and other personal friends, London 1921 (a large volume with full-page colour illustrations)

Dictionary of National Biography Second Supplement Vol II, London 1912

Handbook to the Kate Greenaway Collection with some account of the life and work of Kate Greenaway, London n.d. (contains several illustrations from the collection)

Anne C. Moore, **A Century of Kate Greenaway**, London 1946

Covelle Newcomb, **The Secret Door: The Story of Kate Greenaway** with drawings after her by Addison Burbank, New York 1946

John Ruskin, **The Art of England** Lectures given in Oxford, Lecture IV *Fairy Land,* Orpington 1883 (contains full-page plate of drawings by Kate Greenaway. The lecture praises her work and that of Mrs Allingham)

M.H. Spielmann and G.S. Layard, **Kate Greenaway**, London 1905 (the major biographical work with 140 illustrations, some full-page colour plates and an inaccurate list of some of her works. The original limited edition was issued with a different original sketch in each volume)

M.H. Spielmann, (introduction) **Kate Greenaway** with 16 examples of the artist's work in colour, London 1910 (part of the *British Artists* series)

Biographical Sources—Periodicals

Gazette des Beaux-Arts Vol 1 1882 with an article on Kate Greenaway, Walter Crane and Randolph Caldecott p 74 ff; Vol 3 1910 with an article *Kate Greenaway et ses livres illustrés* pp 5-22

Wide Awake Boston Vol 17 June to Nov 1883 with a short article on her with portrait and illustration *Little Brown Maiden*

The Critic New York Christmas 1885 with the article *Kate Greenaway the Artist: A Review and an Estimate* by M.H. Spielmann with ten drawings, some from rare letters to Ruskin and Violet Dickinson

Illustrations a Magazine of Amusement, Art, Biography conducted by Francis George Heath, London with an article *Art in the Nursery* including 13 drawings by Kate Greenaway

The Pall Mall Budget London 12 Feb 1891 with the article *Kate Greenaway and her Work* with 11 illustrations, her portrait and another shorter article

The Illustrated London News 14 Feb 1891 with an article *Art Exhibitions—The Fine Art Society—Miss Kate Greenaway* p 215 (illustrated with two plates from *Marigold Garden* and one from *Little Anne*)

The Studio London, Extra Christmas Number 1894 contains the Monograph by Gleeson White *Christmas Cards and their Chief Designers* with twelve cards by Kate Greenaway; Extra Christmas Number 1897 contains the Monograph by Gleeson White *Children's Books and their Illustrators* with three illustrations by Kate Greenaway; Vol 136 Sept 1948 an article *Neglected Centenaries* with illustrations pp 75-8

The Tatler London 13 Nov 1901 with the article *The Passing of Miss Kate Greenaway—Friend of Children* including her portrait and some of her work

The Literary Digest New York 7 Dec 1901 containing the article on Kate Greenaway *The Children's Artist* with her portrait; 27

Jan 1906 containing an article *Permanent Qualities of Kate Greenaway's Art* with six of her drawings of children, a portrait in her studio

The American Monthly Review of Reviews New York Dec 1901 containing the article *Kate Greenaway, the Illustrator of Childhood* by Ernest Knaufft with seven of her illustrations and a portrait

The Magazine of Art Vol XXVI Jan 1902 with an article *Kate Greenaway in Memoriam* by M.H. Spielmann pp 118-22

Art Journal New Series London Feb 1902, April 1902 containing Austin Dobson's monograph on Kate Greenaway pp 33-6, pp 105-9 (the article in two parts contains two full-page pencil studies and several reproductions from her books)

The Craftsman London Feb 1905 containing the article *Art in the Home and in the School —A Selection from the Child-Types of Kate Greenaway* pp 519-29 (an interesting illustrated article with line drawings of nursery schoolroom interiors with Greenaway-inspired murals)

Littell's Living Age Boston 23 Dec 1905 containing a short article on Kate Greenaway originally published in the **London Times** as a review of M.H. Spielmann's book *Kate Greenaway* 1905

The Nation 4 Jan 1905 containing a review of *Kate Greenaway* by M.H. Spielmann and G.S. Layard pp 15-6

The Hampstead Annual For 1906-7 containing the article *Reminiscences of Kate Greenaway in Hampstead* by a student friend with two unpublished portraits and a drawing *Study from Life* pp 100-8

Century Magazine New York Dec 1907 containing the article *Kate Greenaway, Friend of Children* by Oliver Locker-Lampson with eight illustrations and her portrait (a delightful account of her personality told by an old acquaintance)

Woman's Home Companion New York Nov 1911 containing an article by Arthur Guiterman, a full-page colour plate *Children Fishing* from a watercolour drawing, a border of children and a portrait of Kate Greenaway

Imprint London 17 Feb 1913 containing the article *The Illustration of Children's Books* by Alice Meynell with a full-page colour plate from *Mother Goose* and woodcuts (with additional pictures by Walter Crane)

The British Museum Quarterly London No 5 Dec 1930 containing the article *Drawings by Kate Greenaway* pp 92-3

Art News New York Vol 37 11 Mar 1939 containing the reproduction *Little Cripple's Complaint* p 11

Apollo London Vol 43 June 1946 containing the article *A Collection of Children's Books Illustrated by Crane, Caldecott and Greenaway* pp 141-3

The Carnegie Magazine Vol 19 Mar 1946 containing the article *Quaint Nostalgic Charm* with the illustration *Polly Put the Kettle On* p 246

Just Buttons Vol 5 No 7 April 1947 containing an article based on the *Trumpeter* by Kate Greenaway pp 181-3; No 11 Aug 1947 containing the article *The Boy at the Stile;* Vol 6 No 3 Dec 1947 with a cover illustration *Willie and Trot*

American Antiques Journal Vol 4 No 11 Nov 1949 the entire issue devoted to the work of Kate Greenaway

Hobbies Vol 55 No 6 Aug 1950 an article *Kate Greenaway—Fairy Limner* pp 16-7; Vol 55 No 7 Sept 1950 an article *Following the Greenaway Trail* pp 16-8; Vol 55 No 10 Dec 1950 an article *Greenaway Christmas Cards* pp 16-7 f; Vol 55 No 12 Feb 1951 an article *The Quiver of Love* pp 88-9 f; Vol 56 No 7 Sept 1951 an article *Glass and China: the Greenaway Nursery* pp 78-81; Vol 57 No 12 Feb 1953 begins a serial *Kate Greenaway's Valentines* pp 20-1; continued March, April, May, June,

July 1953; Vol 58 No 1 Mar 1953 an article *Doll-ology: Kate Greenaway Dolls...* pp 56-7.

The Hampstead Independent Journal Nov 1951 an article *Kate Greenaway—a Hampstead Artist*

Spinning Wheel Vol VII No 12 Dec 1952 an article *Kate Greenaway for the Collector* pp 24-7

American Artist New York Vol 34 Sept 1970 with a reproduced design of an earthenware tile p 60 inspired by Greenaway designs

Burlington Magazine Vol 113 April 1971 with a reproduction of her watercolour *Lucy Locket Lost her Pocket* p xxiv

Connoisseur Vol 177 Aug 1971 with a reproduction of her watercolour *The Fable of the Girl and her Milk Pail* p 309; Vol 179 Feb 1972 an early self-portrait reproduced p 145

Discovering Antiques Part 77 30 Mar 1972 containing an article *The Victorian Nursery: The Books of Crane, Caldecott, Greenaway* by Percy Muir pp 1834-8

Country Life Vol 152 30 Nov 1972 with a reproduction of *Child on a See-Saw* p 1482

Related Source Material

Arsène Alexandre, **L'Art du Rire et la Caricature,** Paris 1893 (p 286 refers to Kate Greenaway

Elizabeth Aslin, **The Aesthetic Movement: Prelude to Art Nouveau,** London 1969

Egerton Castle, **English Book Plates,** London 1892

Ernest D. Chase, **The Romance of Greeting Cards**: an historical account of the origin, evolution and development of Christmas cards, valentines, and other forms of greeting cards from earliest days to present, Dedham, Massachusetts 1956

Ernest Chesneau, **La Peinture Anglaise,** Paris 1881 (English translation 1885)

Mary Clive, **The Day of Reckoning,** London 1964

E.T. Cook and A. Wedderburn, editors, **The Works of John Ruskin,** London 1908

(contains several letters and comments about Kate Greenaway)

Rodney Engen, **Walter Crane as a Book Illustrator,** London 1975

Edmund Evans, **The Reminiscences of Edmund Evans,** edited by Ruari McLean, Oxford 1967 (contains an interesting account of printing techniques and life of the printer)

William Gaunt, **The Aesthetic Adventure,** London 1945

Ruth W. Lee, **A History of Valentines,** London 1953

E.V. Lucas, **A Wanderer in London,** London 1906 (contains three pages on Kate Greenaway and Hampstead)

Percy Muir, **Victorian Illustrated Books,** London 1971 (contains a chapter on Kate Greenaway and Walter Crane)

Gerald Reitlinger, **The Economics of Taste** Vol 1, London 1961

John Ruskin, **Praeterita,** an autobiographical work issued in 28 parts, 24 of which were collected in two volumes, London 1885-9 (also a 1900 edition) (with several references to Kate Greenaway)

Charles Spencer, **The Aesthetic Movement,** London 1973

Frank Staff, **The Valentine and its Origins,** London 1969

Sir Charles Tennyson, **Alfred Tennyson, Frederick Locker and Augustine Birrell,** a talk delivered to the Rowfant Club, Cleveland Ohio 1965

Stanley Weintraub, **Beardsley,** London 1967